What constitutes the nature of true love? is an important question for everyone as family, friends and well-wishers gather to celebrate a wedding.

At some point in the wedding service a question will be asked that is blunt, profound, scary, and all encompassing:

"Will you love, comfort, honour and protect, and, forsaking all others, be faithful as long as you both shall live?"

The exact words may vary, but the couple are being asked to make a binding, absolute promise to love one another "till death us do part".

Can you promise to love!? *Is that how true love works?*

Ask most people to define love and they would talk about romance or feelings. Red roses, soft lighting and slow dancing. It's the tingle down the spine, the weakening of the knees, the sweaty palms, the excited giggle. True love, we think, is about these powerful, uncontrollable emotions. You know it's love when the chemistry kicks in. We know it's love when we get a gut feeling that confirms everything on first contact:

> *"It's in his kiss (that's where it is)"*

And if you want to show your love for someone, then you do something romantic. You give them chocolates. You share a candlelit dinner. You walk together in the moonlight.

As wonderful as they are, there is a problem with romance and feelings. Romance and feelings draw people together. But while they are an important part of launching a married relationship, they are a very poor basis for *maintaining* a marriage long term.

Feelings don't serve us well as a definition of love. Sometimes I feel strongly about my children. I feel protective or affectionate. They fill me with joy and delight. They make me proud and glad to be their father. *But at other times…* Well, let's just say they leave me feeling frustrated and hurt.

But that doesn't mean I have stopped loving them.

Feelings are great, but they're not a good guide to true love. They come and go with our moods. They can be affected by illness, the seasons, fatigue. True love is something that goes beyond a feeling. And it has to be more if it is going to last "till death us do part".

So what is true love? And how can you tell when you've found it? The Bible tells us what love is ~ not in some dry, philosophical way, but in a very practical way. It tells us that human love is a pale reflection of the love that God has for each one of us. It tells us that, even if we do not recognise him, God is the source and model of all the love we experience or yearn for.

And it tells us that we see this love most clearly in his Son, Jesus Christ. In Jesus, God shows us what true love is. The Bible explains:

> *But God shows his great love for us in this way: Christ died for us while we were still sinners.* Romans 5 v 8

What is true love?

Jesus revealed the love of God in his *life*. He was filled with compassion for those in need. He was a committed, caring friend to those around him. He shed tears of grief at the death of his friend. But it was in Jesus' *death* that we see the full extent of God's love.

God the Father gave his own Son. God gave what was most precious to him ~ he gave the Son he loves.

Jesus' death was not an accident. Neither was he a victim. He died *willingly*. It was Roman soldiers who executed him in the first century by nailing him to a wooden cross. But he didn't have his life taken from him against his will. No, *he gave up his life.* He went willingly to his death. The love that Jesus showed to us is costly. True love, we discover, involves sacrifice.

And Jesus Christ died *for us.* His death wasn't an empty gesture. His death had a purpose ~ a purpose that arose from God's love for us. Jesus Christ died *to save us.* He died to give us life and hope. The Bible continues:

But God shows his great love for us in this way: Christ died for us while we were still sinners. So through Christ we will surely be saved from God's anger, because we have been made right with God by the blood of Christ's death. While we were God's enemies, he made us his friends through the death of his Son. Surely, now that we are his friends, he will save us through his Son's life. Romans 5 v 8-10

Jesus Christ's death does two things; something in the present and something in the future.

In the present the death of Jesus can make us right with God.

We've all rejected God. We've chosen to live our lives without him. And that means we've made ourselves God's enemies. That's true of everyone. It doesn't matter how good you are or how religious you are. The reality is that we've all become God's enemies.

But Jesus can make us right with God. We're God's enemies, but God sent Jesus to make peace. Through Jesus we can be friends with God.

In the future the death of Jesus can save us from judgment. Jesus, the most loving person who ever lived, taught clearly and consistently about the reality of God's anger against sin. God is not indifferent to the suffering and hurt we've caused. He's committed to justice. So a day is coming when God will judge all people ~ including you and me. Jesus did not stay dead. He rose from the grave and is alive today. His resurrection is the guarantee that he can give us life beyond death.

But God is also committed to love. In his love he sent Jesus so we can be "justified"; declared innocent of all the wrongs we have done. Jesus died in our place. He took the punishment for sin that we deserve on himself. He was judged instead of us, so we can go free. If Jesus reconciles us to God now, we can be sure that Jesus will save us from God's coming judgment.

This is true love. True love is sacrificial. True love gives up everything. True love gives up even life itself. This is God's demonstration of true love: Jesus Christ died in our place to reconcile us to God.

The wedding service doesn't ask, *"Do you love?"* as though it is asking the couple to say how they are feeling *right now*. It asks *"Will you love?"* Are you determined to pursue and work out your commitment and promise to love in practical, everyday life ~ whatever the cost?

At a wedding, the couple commit themselves to love one another, until they are separated by death. But the good news of the Christian message is that the death of Jesus Christ unites us to God. And the resurrection of Jesus shows us that this is a union that will go on beyond death and last for all eternity.

How God proves his love

When did God love us? While we were still sinners. While we were his enemies. What is true love? What is God's love like? God loves his enemies.

When we were unable to help ourselves, at the right time, Christ died for us, although we were living against God. Very few people will die to save the life of someone else. Although perhaps for a good person someone might pos-

sibly die. But God shows his great love for us in this way: Christ died for us while we were still sinners.
Romans 5 v 6-8

Who would you die for? You might die for your wife or husband. You might die for your children. You might die for a friend. Some of us might die for our country or a cause we really believe in. *We might.*

It's hard to know for sure until we actually face that kind of choice. But Jesus' death is something completely different. It reveals a love beyond anything we imagine: *"Christ died for us while we were still sinners".*

God the Son died for rebels, for the powerless, for the ungodly. That's what marks out true love.

There was nothing in us to make God love us. We are usually drawn to people who are a bit like us. But God loved the ungodly ~ those who were not like him at all. We look for relationships with people who can give us something: affection, support, security. But there was nothing we could bring to a relationship with God: we were powerless. There was nothing in us to make God love us.

Yet God loved us. Jesus Christ didn't just die. He died *for sinners*, for his enemies, for the ungodly.

The great thing about this is that it includes *everyone*. No one need be left out. Christianity is not just for good people or clever people, or attractive people or religious people. Jesus is for people like you and me. Everyone is welcome. God's love is for you. The love of God, demonstrated in the death of his Son, is for you ~ if you will receive it.

A love that never ends

Romance is wonderful and feelings are great. But love needs promises to survive the ups and downs of life. We make wedding vows because sooner or later we're going to let one another down. In those moments our promises help love survive.

In the same way, God gives us promises. He promises that when we stand before God, and all our selfish faults and failings are exposed, he will go on loving us for all eternity.

Even the best marriages come to an end. *"Till death us do part"* is a reminder that death does part us. But God offers us a love that never ends. This love will never end because it never runs out. God loved us when we were at our worst ~ when we were his enemies.

And this love will never end because God's love has conquered death. Jesus Christ not only died. He rose again, and is alive today. We will "be saved through his life!" Christ's death is the demonstration of a love without limit. His new life is the promise of a love that never ends.

If you want to be reconciled with God, then all you need to do is turn to him. He's ready to welcome you

~ of course he is, because he's already given his Son for you. You can express trust in Jesus Christ by praying this prayer:

> *Father God, thank you for your love.*
> *I'm sorry that I've not loved you as I should.*
> *I'm sorry that I've made myself your enemy.*
> *But I thank you that you carried on loving me.*
> *Thank you sending your Son, Jesus Christ.*
> *Thank you that he died in my place.*
> *Thank you for his resurrection and the promise of eternal love.*
> *Help me to trust in him and enjoy your love.*
> *Amen.*